A Splintered Mirror

Chinese Poetry
from the Democracy Movement

Translated by Donald Finkel

Additional Translations by Carolyn Kizer

North Point Press · San Francisco · 1991

Library of Congress Cataloging-in-Publication Data
A Splintered mirror : Chinese poetry from the
  democracy movement / translated by Donald
  Finkel ; additional translations by Carolyn Kizer.
      p.   cm.
  ISBN 0-86547-448-6. — ISBN 0-86547-449-4
  (pbk.)
  1. Chinese poetry—20th century—Translations into
  English. 2. English poetry—Translations from
  Chinese. 3. Democracy—Poetry. I. Finkel, Donald.
PL2658.E3S67 1991
895.1'15208—dc20   90-7349

North Point Press
850 Talbot Avenue
Berkeley, California
94706

Contents

Acknowledgments

Some of these translations have appeared in *American Poetry Review*, *Antaeus*, *Delos*, *Folio*, *Ironwood*, *Literary Review*, *Manoa*, *Poetry East*, *Poetry*, and *Seneca Review*. A version of the preface also appeared in *Delos*.

Shu Ting's "The Singing Flower," "Missing You," and "Bits of Reminiscence" were included in *Carrying Over* by Carolyn Kizer, Copper Canyon Press, 1988.

These translations would never have seen the light of day without the invaluable assistance of Chang Sheng-Tai, Chen Xueliang, Li Guohua, Yi Jinsheng, and Y. H. Zhao. I am also greatly indebted to Bonnie McDougall, whose translations have had so much to do with introducing the work of the Misty Poets (especially that of Bei Dao) to readers of English. Finally, I should like to express my gratitude to Qiu Xiaolong, Jerome Seaton, John Balcom, and Barbara Ras.

About the Translations

Bei Dao's poems were translated by Donald Finkel with Chen Xueliang; Duo Duo's with Li Guohua; Gu Cheng's "Capital 'I,'" "Parting," "A Headstrong Boy," "Winter Longing," and "Image" (in preface) with Yi Jinsheng; "Ark," "Dream Garden," "Black-and-White Sketches," and "Yesterday" with Li Guohua; "A Crack," "Rebel Camp in the Hindu Kush," "When Hope Comes Back," and "When I Blink" with Chang Sheng-Tai; Jiang He's "Unfinished Poem" with Yi Jinsheng; "Dividing the Sky" and "Chasing the Sun" with Li Guohua; Mang Ke's "These Days," "Old Age," and "Sorrows" with Chang Sheng-Tai; "A Fallen Tree" and "After the Night" with Li Guohua; Yang Lian's "Nuo-ri-lang" with Li Guohua.

The poems of Shu Ting were translated by Carolyn Kizer with Y. H. Zhao, with the exception of "Also All" and "Fairy Tales," which were translated by Donald Finkel with Yi Jinsheng.

Preface: A Crown of Flowers

Image

The sky is grey.
The road is grey.
The buildings are grey.
The rain is grey.

Out of the dead grey void
two children walk,
one bright red
and one light green.

In 1980, when Gu Cheng published this brief lyric in the *Poetry Monthly*, an official critic called it "misty." Even his father, the poet Gu Gong, protested he couldn't understand it. In time, there began to appear a veritable cloud of "misty poets" to befuddle the innocent. Judged from the perspective of socialist realism and party rhetoric, Gu Cheng's poem may indeed have seemed elusive—though for an American reader it might have struck a familiar chord, recalling those early imagist vignettes that recalled in turn the classical Chinese poems to which Fenollosa and Pound had long ago introduced us. But, reading it in the context of the following quotation, which appeared the year before in the manifesto of another new literary magazine, the critic may well have glimpsed an ominous shape in the mist. This heavily ironic passage is drawn from Karl Marx's "Comments on the Latest Prussian Censorship Instruction," written almost 150 years ago.

> You admire the delightful variety, the inexhaustible riches of nature. You do not demand that the rose should smell like the violet, but must the greatest riches of all, the spirit, exist in only *one* variety? I am humorous, but the law bids me write seriously. I am audacious, but the law commands that my style be modest. *Grey, all grey*, is the sole, the rightful color of freedom. Every drop of dew on which the sun shines glistens with an inexhaustible play of

colors, but the spiritual sun, however many the persons and whatever the objects in which it is refracted, must produce only the *official color*! The most essential form of the spirit is *cheerfulness, light*, but you make *shadow* the sole manifestation of the spirit; it must be clothed only in black, yet among flowers there are no black ones.

It has been suggested that Misty poetry may have had its genesis in the *Tiananmen Anthology*, which grew out of a mass demonstration in Tiananmen Square in April 1976 to mourn the death of Chou Enlai and to protest against the dictatorship of Mao Zedong and the Gang of Four. In a grim foreshadowing of the events of June 1989, the demonstrators were violently dispersed. But the anthology was clandestinely preserved, and probably had something to do with the blossoming of the democracy movement in China.

It may be difficult for an American reader (raised in a country where, as Adrienne Rich puts it, "poets don't go to jail / for being poets") to conceive of Gu Cheng's mild observation as political commentary—but after the dismal, violent, self-righteous excesses of the Cultural Revolution, even the publication of a simple love poem might have constituted for the official critic an expression of anti-socialist individualism. He may have understood well enough—there was a thorny flower barely shrouded in the mist. Still, there was no need to call attention to it. The crime of obscurity was sufficiently audacious. Even today, in official circles, the failure of *meng-lung shih*, or "misty poetry," to communicate, to rouse the ardor of the masses for the Four Modernizations, is recognized as an offense against socialist morality. The utterances of these poets—Gu Cheng's stubborn, headstrong dreams, Shu Ting's invincible affections, Bei Dao's solitary vigils on unfamiliar shores—are tinged with the same defiance as, say, Jiang He's vision of triumphant martyrdom at the conclusion of his "Unfinished Poem."

Periods of political repression have often, and for various reasons, evoked complex poetic responses. Sometimes the motive behind the "mistiness" of these poems appears to have originated simply as veiled criticism or covert resistance. However, with time and distance, the disguise begins to take on a life of its own, and what may have begun as protective ambiguity is transformed by imperceptible stages into outright ambivalence. In other circumstances, the initial impulse itself seems charged with ambivalence, the expression of a species of lovers' quarrel between poet and polis. In fact, if there is anything unexpected for an American reader, it is a persistent optimism in the face of that grim official grey—a stubbornly Marxist faith in the millennium. Even the often gloomy Gu Cheng admits as much to his sister poet, Shu Ting:

> Outside, the sun will anchor in the harbor.
> The East will redden, blushing, little by little.
> She'll have caught sight of the world
> and fallen in love like a schoolgirl.
> The dripping bush will be crowned with flowers.

But the primary affirmation of these poets is their allegiance to poetry itself, to the power of boldly delineated personal imagery to render communicable truths—or, as in some of the poems of Jiang He and of Yang Lian, to the ancient and unsuppressible impulse of myth. Didn't Chairman Mao say it—"Let a hundred flowers bloom"? Misty flowers these may be, but certainly not black ones or grey ones. "Bright sunflower petals fall like random notes," Gu Cheng sings, "the melody dispersing like some imperial family / at the end of a long grey corridor of space and time." "The oranges are ripe," Bei Dao assures his readers, though "bitter threads web every / sun-drenched segment."

Biographical Notes

Bei Dao (1949–): Pen name of Zhao Zhenkai.* One of the leading figures among the Misty Poets, if not the most significant, he has published fiction and translations as well. Together with Mang Ke, in 1978, he founded the short-lived but ground-breaking journal *Today*, which he is now in the process of resurrecting. In recent years he has taught and lectured in Great Britain and the United States. He is currently living in Norway.

Duo Duo (1951–): Pen name of Li Shizheng. One of the important precursors of Misty poetry, he has also published a number of short stories. For some time he worked as a reporter for *The Peasant Daily* in Beijing. He is now in England, teaching at London University.

Gu Cheng (1956–): Youngest of the Misties, he is the son of the poet Gu Gong. He and his family were driven to the countryside in 1969. He returned to Beijing in 1974 and set to work as a carpenter. By 1979 his first poems began to appear anonymously. He is living in New Zealand.

Jiang He (1949–): Pen name of Yu Yuze. One of the central figures among the Misties. During the Cultural Revolution, he was arrested and maltreated, primarily for the alleged political crimes of his father. After his early expressions of political protest, he turned to poetic recreations of traditional Chinese mythology. He lives in New York City and is working on a novel.

Mang Ke (1951–): Pen name of Jiang Shi-wei. Another precursor of Misty poetry, he was a co-founder of the underground poetry journal

* The use of pen names during the Cultural Revolution could not help taking on a political significance. Many of the poems in this collection were first published and distributed in secrecy, sometimes posted on walls to be read furtively, before being torn down by the authorities.

Today. Shortly after the massacre in Tiananmen Square on June 4, 1989, he was arrested by the authorities.

Shu Ting (1952–): Pen name of Gong Peiyu. Removed from Beijing during the Cultural Revolution, she went to live in a distant peasant village, where she began to write poetry. Within about ten years she had achieved such a reputation that even the official critics were compelled to recognize her. She won the National Poetry Award in both 1981 and 1983. She is now a member of the Chinese Writers' Association and lives in Xiamen.

Yang Lian (1955–): Another widely published Misty Poet. A member of the Chinese Writers' Association, he worked a while for the Chinese Broadcast Ensemble in Beijing. At present he is living in New Zealand.

A Splintered Mirror

BEI DAO

Let's Go

Let's go,
dry leaves blowing down the valley,
homeless, singing.

Let's go,
moonlight on river ice,
overflowing.

Let's go,
watching the same patch of sky,
hearts drumming in the dusk.

Let's go.
We know by heart
the way to the fountainhead.

Let's go
down the road, strolling through drifts
of scarlet poppies.

Memory

Candlelight flickered
on every face
and left no wake.

Shadows brushed
the snowy walls
like dark spindrift.

On the wall
a hanging guitar
sounds dimly

like rigging lights
whispering together
on quiet water.

Notes on the City of the Sun

LIFE
It rises, like the sun.

LOVE
A flock of geese floats quietly
across the desolate virgin land.
An old tree crashes.
A salty rain falls in the silence.

FREEDOM
Tiny scraps of paper
drift on the wind.

CHILD
Inside, a picture of the ocean folds
into a snowy dove.

GIRL
A rainbow gathers
trembling feathers from the sky.

YOUTH
Red waves drown
a lonely oar.

ART
In a splintered mirror blaze
a thousand suns.

PEOPLE
Scattered into grains of shining wheat,
the moon's broadcast across
the open sky, the innocent land.

LABOR

One hand encircles
the whole round earth.

FATE

A small boy rattles a stick along a railing.
An unlatched gate bangs in the windy night.

FAITH

Legions of sheep pour from the grassy pasture
while the shepherd pipes a dismal tune on his flute.

PEACE

At the emperor's tomb
a rusting musket sprouts a fresh green twig
to make a crutch for some crippled veteran.

MOTHERLAND

Wrought on an old bronze shield, she leans
in a dusty corner of the museum.

LIFE

A net.

Answer

The scoundrel carries his baseness around like an ID card.
The honest man bears his honor like an epitaph.
Look—the gilded sky is swimming
with undulant reflections of the dead.

They say the ice age ended years ago.
Why are there icicles everywhere?
The Cape of Good Hope has already been found.
Why should all those sails contend on the Dead Sea?

I came into this world with nothing
but paper, rope, and shadow.
Now I come to be judged,
and I've nothing to say but this:

Listen. *I don't believe!*
OK. You've trampled
a thousand enemies underfoot. Call me
a thousand and one.

I don't believe the sky is blue.
I don't believe what the thunder says.
I don't believe dreams aren't real,
that beyond death there is no reprisal.

If the sea should break through the sea-wall,
let its brackish water fill my heart.
If the land should rise from the sea again,
we'll choose again to live in the heights.

The earth revolves. A glittering constellation
pricks the vast defenseless sky.
Can you see it there? that ancient ideogram—
the eye of the future, gazing back.

All

All is fated,
all cloudy,

all an endless beginning,
all a search for what vanishes,

all joys grave,
all griefs tearless,

every speech a repetition,
every meeting a first encounter,

all love buried in the heart,
all history prisoned in a dream,

all hope hedged with doubt,
all faith drowned in lamentation.

Every explosion heralds an instant of stillness,
every death reverberates forever.

Unfamiliar Shore

1

These sails are slack.
These masts, like winter wood, contrive
an unlikely spring.

2

The crumbling lighthouse cups at least
a memory of light.

On the ruined stair,
running your knuckles along the rusty railing,
you play a dreary tune.

3

In the solemn noon, shadows withdraw
to their narrow rooms.

Salt fills every crevice,
crystallized by yesterday's chill,
by memory's flickering, scintillant light.

4

Far out, a vast white waste.

Onto the shore, like a floating deck,
spray how many nets of sleepy foam?

5

Like a red scarf, that bird soars out
across the Sea of Japan.

The firelight throws your silhouette
against an unconditional blue

backdrop of sky.
No storm in sight. The wind's not sure
which way to blow.
As if in answer, wings
whir like bowstrings overhead.

6

Fold on fold, the tide flows out,
spilling on a golden carpet
the foamy evening, exposing here
a loosening hawser, there a broken oar.

Bare to the waist, some fishermen strain
to rebuild a storm-torn temple.

7

Children chase the crescent moon.

A gull swoops down, but will not light
on your outstretched hand.

A Ticket

He hasn't got a ticket.
How can he get aboard?
The anchor chain grinds and rumbles,
alarming the night.

Oh the sea, the sea. In the slackening tide,
an island looms, lonely as a heart.
No soft shadows from dooryard hedges,
no plumes from kitchen chimneys.

The mast that drew lightning is struck again,
to splinters. Countless storms have left
their prints on fish-scales, sea-shells,
the jellyfish's delicate umbrella.
Waves pass the ancient tale from crest to crest.

He hasn't got a ticket.

Oh the sea, the sea, heaped on mossy reefs,
scatters in the naked midnight.
Gull feathers glimmer on moonlit water.
Tritons and mermaids begin to sing
as the tide subsides.

He hasn't got a ticket.

Time won't stop for him, though.
Ready to cast off, a sunken ship is firing her boilers,
rekindling crimson flames. As the waves rear,
the eyes of the dead flicker fitfully in the depths.

He hasn't got a ticket.

Oh dazzling, dazzling,
that reach of sunlight drying on the sand.

He hasn't got a ticket.

Testament

Perhaps the time has come.
I haven't left a will,
just one pen, for my mother.

I'm no hero, you understand.
This isn't the year for heroes.
I'd just like to be a man.

The horizon still divides
the living from the dead,
but the sky's all I need.

I won't kneel on the earth—
the firing squad might block
the last free breaths of air.

From starry bullet-holes
the blood-red dawn will flow.

Transparent Grief

My transparent grief
was filled with you
as though the night's green mist
had swathed itself about a lonely tree.

You tore that mist to tatters, bit by bit,
with icy fingers,
taking it gently in
as though you were drinking flimsy veils of milk.

Now you breathe out
a golden moon
that rises, slowly,
bathing the road in light.

Love Story

After all, there's only one world for us—
the height of summer.
Yet we go on playing children's games
with grown-up rules,
heedless of those fallen by the roadside,
heedless of the ships that have run aground.

The sun that warms the lovers
heaps the haggard, pitch-black night
on the laborer's back.
Even on the path where the lovers meet,
some day an icy wind will blow
as enemies come face to face.

This is no longer a simple story.
There's you and me.
And there are other people.

The Oranges Are Ripe

The oranges are ripe.
Dripping with sun, the oranges
are ready.
          Let me
walk into your heart,
heavy with love.

The oranges are ripe.
The rind sprays
a delicate mist.
                    Let me
walk into your heart,
my grief dissolving
into blissful tears.

The oranges are ripe.
Bitter threads web every
sun-drenched segment.
                         Let me
walk into your heart to gather
my dismembered dream.

The oranges are ripe,
dripping with sun. The oranges
are ready.

Snow Line

Forget what I said.
Forget the bird shot from the sky.
Forget the crags,
let them go under again.

Forget the sun, even.
In that eternal place
burns a lamp of dust.

Above the snow line
after the avalanches,
something is quietly
healing on the cliff.

Below the snow line
meltwater streams
through the lush marsh grass.

Accomplices

After all those years
mica glints in the mud,
evil as it is bright,
tiny suns in vipers' eyes.

Branch roads appear and disappear
in the hands of trees.
Where did that fawn go?
Only cemeteries could assuage
this desolation, like tiny cities.

Freedom is only the distance
between the hunter and his prey.
As we turn to look,
a bat describes a sweeping arc
across the vast canvas of our inheritance
and vanishes into the dusk.

Nor are we free of guilt.
Long since, in history's mirror,
we became accomplices,
awaiting the day we might
seep down through the layers of stone
into subterranean pools
to contemplate darkness again.

Elegy

A widow offers her broken tears to an idol.
A pack of newborn wolves waits to be fed,
who fled the death march one by one.
Shrugging, the mountain echoes my lament.
Together we surround the farm

from which you came, where the smoke
winds from the chimney into the sky
and wreaths of wild chrysanthemums
drift on the wind.

In the wheat field when we met
you thrust your small hard breasts at me.
Wheat sprang madly from the stones.
Now you're that widow. What's been lost

is me—and this glorious lifelong desire
to lie together, sweating torrents,
our bed adrift on morning's river.

Many Years

It's you, it's you,
perplexed by flickering shadows,
now bright, now dim—
it's you to whom
I can no longer go.
Now even the cold frustrates me.

For many years,
before the icebergs came,
fish rose and sank—
for many years.

Stepping carefully, I make my way
through the swirling night.
Lamps glow on prongs of steel.

For many years,
in the desolate room,
without a clock, without a key
(the last ones must have
taken that too)—I lived,
for many years.

Someone whistles in the mist.
The train rattles past on the bridge.

Season after season set out
from the little country station,
pausing a moment at every tree,
which blossomed and bore fruit
for many years.

The Window in the Cliff

The wasp arouses the flower with terrible thrusts.
Today, of all days in the year, the letter's been sent.
Damp matches no longer light my way.
Wolves prowl among people turned to trees.
Snowdrifts melt all at once. On my watch dial
winter keeps its fitful silence.

What bores through the rock is not pure water.
Hacked off with an axe, the chimney smoke
stands upright in the air.
Tiger stripes of sunlight glide down the wall.
Stones grow and dreams roam aimlessly.
Here and there in the undergrowth, life climbs
in search of speech while stars explode.

In heat, the river drives toward the city
a rubble of rusty shells. Menacing brambles
spring up in the ditches.
In the market, women are buying spring.

The August Sleepwalker

On the sea-floor a stone bell, tolling,
tolling, roils the waves.

It's August tolling.
That isn't the noon-high August sun,

it's a sail billowing with milk
over floating corpses.

It's August billowing,
August apples tumbling from the heights.

Now the long-dead beacon's
agleam with sailors' eyes.

It's August gleaming,
a country fair, presaging the first frost.

On the sea-floor a stone bell, tolling,
tolling, roils the waves.

The August sleepwalker has seen
the midnight sun.

DUO DUO

When the People Arose from Cheese

The songs ignored the blood of revolution.
August tautened like a cruel bow.

The malevolent son strode from the hut
with a pouch of tobacco and a parched throat.

Cruelly blinded, oxen dragged
blackening corpses behind them
like distended drums,
till all the sacrifices had been hidden away.

In the distance, another legion approaches.

Saying Good-bye

The green field stretches out like a mind at ease,
like a construction, like an interminable evening,
while the future marches toward you like a legion.

It's as if, on the desolate path to maturity,
you've been forced toward some unfamiliar crossing.
All the lights are out.

Only one shepherd, clutching a bright red whip.
Oh, he's just guarding the night,
just guarding the darkness.

The blood of one entire class . . .

The blood of one entire class has already been shed.
The archers of one entire class are still shooting
at the vacant banal sky,
that ancient, interminable Chinese dream,
while a sour grey moon
rises above the deserted shore of history.

In this pitch-dark, desolate city
again the red terror begins
its savage hammering.

Summer

The flowers are blooming still, those hypocrites.
The ferocious trees go on shaking and shaking,
endlessly dropping their luckless offspring to the ground.

Backing off like a boxer, the sun's already
crept over the wall, leaving the young man alone
among the woebegone sunflowers.

Night

In the night, awash with symbols,
the moon seems like the ashen face of an invalid,
like delusive, fleeting time,
like death, like a doctor at a bedside.

A few tired emotions,
a few awful moments of uncertainty.

Moonlight coughs in the dooryard.
Moonlight, oh, sharp intimation of exile.

From Death's Point of View

Looking from death's point of view
you'll see people you'd
never see in your life.

For a time you'll wander,
sniffing here and there.
Then you'll bury yourself
at the very heart of their hatred.

They'll shovel dust in your face.
You should be grateful—
doubly grateful.

You'll never see your enemies again,
nor hear again
those malevolent screams,
those screams that freeze your spine.

Gallery

A

The fog creeps blindly onward, pulling out of the station.
Little by little, day is breaking.
Meanwhile, beyond the horizon, where the dirt road loses itself
among dark, fallow fields, it is turning dusk.

B

Caught without his clothes, the clumsy lover
pecks fretfully at the bark
and scatters splinters with his beak,
as the hunter, clutching his terrible gun,
draws shut the meshes of the evening.

C

She stands, this morning, dew scattered in her hair,
gazing at the vineyard like a lady inspecting her garden,
smiling on it—with a dash of trampled sweetness,
and a delicate hint of grief.

D

Waking happily, as if in your own house,
seeing the wall adazzle in the setting sun,
you wrap yourself in a striped bath towel,
lift up your bare arms and begin
to comb your hair.

E

Caroling loudly, baring her lovely throat,
gathering in her basket the fallen stars,
she strolls into the depths of the forest,
singing, singing an age-old tale.

F

Look! A windowful of sunlight on my palette,
my musket, and my bachelor's cot.
Oh, you are coming,
even as I wait.

G

Night falls.
Your words of refusal
are dripping with innocence.
Your hair is snagged on the dusk
and your eyes fill with darkness.
Not a glimmer of light.

H

Oh yes, the night
has hidden your face
and altered your voice.
I can feel
our love now,
gliding silently
like a sleigh
across a wound.

GU CHENG

Capital "I"

I stare into the sun, at the bright dawn.
Whirling toward me like a dagger,
like a prismatic intangible vision,
like a fantastic sea, it dazzles me.
Who says metal doesn't dream?
Who says blood doesn't yearn?
I want to run, to cry out,
to stand gazing at this sea,
which covers half a continent.

A cold gleaming joy, a rising shimmer of heat,
sends me galloping across mountains
as if across a keyboard,
each step raising sudden echoes.
Bright sunflower petals fall like random notes,
the melody dispersing like some imperial family
at the end of a long grey corridor of space and time.
Gaping, I inhale the sun. It leaves on the sky
one pale thumbprint called the moon.

This boundless energy sends me
down the winding green yarn of a riverbank,
tracing a formless orbit.
The heat of my passion dissipates in the four directions,
riffling the radiant purple curtain of the sky.

Matter's dissolving now,
it's drifting toward me—not like a wave,
like an enormous cloud of kisses and embraces.
This buoyant joy dissolves me into a thousand
shapes and colors, molecules, sugars, acids, proteins.
In the tangled seaweed, floating like a soft appalling cloud,
swim frogs and fishes, as life turns slowly vertebrate.

Then, from the curves of avoidance and pursuit,
the manifold strategies of camouflage
evolve hot blood, cold blood.

Oh, I laugh at death, that ragged curtain
which will never come down on my miracle play.
I'm all humanity, stalking the long corridors of time,
climbing the multicolored cliffs of every continent.
Rivers carry my songs,
earthquakes scatter my bones,
rainclouds rinse my hair.
I'm a black boy, wearing a stolen anklet of iron.
I'm a brown girl, polishing the slim throat of an urn.
I'm a snowman, snared in a net of speculation.

No! I'm golden as a harvest,
as a ripe tangerine among green leaves.
I'm fresh-mown hay, a shore of exploding sand.
I'm golden. Every golden evening,
gilding the inscriptions on crude monuments,
my dreams engender history.

Perhaps, as the time approaches, I'll grow silent.
I'll rise again and again,
like the sun from the fathomless sea,
announcing to the world, in the voice of the spectrum,
rearranging all the characters and the words:
The East is merely a myth no longer!

Parting

Now, as we cross this ancient threshold,
let's have no farewells,
no valedictions.

They seem so hollow—
silence is best.
Reticence is no pretense.

Let's bequeath our memory to the future,
our dreams to the night,
our tears to the sea,
and our windy sighs to its sails.

A Headstrong Boy

I guess my mother spoiled me—
I'm a headstrong boy. I want every instant
to be lovely as crayons.

I'd like to draw—on chaste white paper—
a clumsy freedom, eyes that never wept,
a piece of sky, a feather, a leaf,
a pale green evening, and an apple.

I'd like to draw dawn, the smile dew sees,
the earliest, tenderest love—an imaginary love
who's never seen a mournful cloud,
whose eyes the color of sky will gaze at me
forever, and never turn away.
I'd like to draw distance, a bright horizon,
carefree, rippling rivers, hills sheathed in green furze.
I want the lovers to stand together in silence,
I want each breathless moment to beget a flower.

I want to draw a future I've never seen—
nor ever can—though I'm sure she'll be beautiful.
I'll draw her an autumn coat the color of candle flame,
and maple leaves, and all the hearts that ever loved her.
I'll draw her a wedding, an early morning garden party,
swathed in candy-wrappers decked with winter scenes.

I'm a headstrong boy. I want to paint out every sorrow,
to cover the world with colored windows,
let all the eyes accustomed to darkness
be accustomed to light. I want to draw wind,
mountains, each one bigger than the last.
I want to draw the dream of the East,
a fathomless sea, a joyful voice.

Finally, I'd like to draw myself in one corner—
a panda, huddled in a dark Victorian forest,
hunkering in the quiet branches, homeless, lost,
not even a heart left behind me, far away,
only teeming dreams of berries
and great, wide eyes.

This pining's pointless.
I haven't any crayons,
any breathless moments.
All I have are fingers and pain.

I think I'll tear the paper to bits
and let them drift away,
hunting for butterflies.

Ark

The ship you've boarded
is doomed to go under—
vanish into the breathing sea.

But you still have time to stare at the flag,
or at the dark, unfolding plain,
or at the white birds twittering
over their watery grave.

You still have time to lean on the rail,
puzzled by a sound in the passageway—
though the whole ship is empty,
though every door is ajar—

till cool flames float up
from every cabin.

Winter Longing

In the naked tree an enormous crow,
black as the night a moment
before daybreak, blinks
one eye, then
the other, gleaming
against the cloudless silent sky.

A longing—
a moody longing—
goads me through haggard shadows,
trampling the dry clods.
Are there no tadpoles anywhere,
wriggling, searching for green coral?

Autumn

Autumn's a blue country
where blue birds perch on the roads
while leaves and crumpled bills
flutter into the sky.

It's shining out there.
The sun's put on his hat.
It's deserted out there.
Sometimes you can hear the sound
of falling snow.

Out there
the destination sign will fall
from the side of my railroad car.

A Crack

Hidden among boards and stones,
a crack
beckons the inquisitive eye.
Sound of a cylinder revolving,
the bead held steady, the breath held still.

Spring is buzzing.
Seeds hunt for the sun.
A centipede dangles like a spring,
then vanishes.

Rebel Camp in the Hindu Kush

The mountains lie quietly together
like packs of shaggy camels
under the stars.

The campfires multiply.

Guarding his homeland, a partisan
raises a shepherd's tune
from an empty cartridge case.

On the horizon
not one single light.

Dream Garden

We slip into a dream
to shelter from the rain.
Our umbrella's made of paper
as red as your smile.

We look at each other
and at the black poplars
where birds are perching.

Now and then, a flash of lightning.

Last time I was here alone
after the rain
a bog spread out around me
on every side.

Through it, a river ran,
cold blood gleaming
from its mouth.

When Hope Comes Back
for Shu Ting

There's nothing left.

The southwest wind's already landed.
The sky's alive with gulls.
The evening's shaken out the waves,
folded one hapless mast neatly in two.
Flounder swim imperturbably,
uninvited, through the skull of a ship.
Gleaming like coins, their eyes recall
an army of shopkeepers.

There's nothing left.

The lamp turns to a firefly in my hand
and darts through the darkness. The last patient candle
topples to the ground, kindling a cry of delight.
A fire blazes up and spreads until
the child who before was afraid of the dark
now shrieks at this strange conflagration and scampers home.
Curled in a ball, he hides one spark in his dream
while, humming softly, his mother closes the shutters.

There's nothing left.

The sea is black as a hole,
the squid's insidious ink swirls into the sky,
the screaming seagulls urge the storm clouds on.
Only the tree can't fly. Stricken by lightning,
thrashing its tormented feathers,
the olive tree wants to demolish the sky.

There's nothing left.

Nothing? Really?
Tell me. The warm earth shimmers.
"There's more," you say, in your low, melodious voice
as the river trembles in a lightning flash
and vanishes. "There's more."
As if the world were a small black boy
who'd wept too long, you comfort him
like an older sister, and smooth his dripping hair.

"There's more."

You whisper it in his ear while the world sleeps calmly,
while motherless birds crowd sleeping together
and the sea leans against the shoulder of the cliff.
He sleeps on quietly. Quietly.
From far away, a solitary star approaches.
It wants to stand beneath his window on the lawn
and learn how to commune with the taciturn grass.

"There's more. More."
The world will wake at daybreak, fully grown.
His eyes will flash a grown-up smile. Yes.
Outside, the sun will anchor in the harbor.
The East will redden, blushing, little by little.
She'll have caught sight of the world
and fallen in love like a schoolgirl.
The dripping bush will be crowned with flowers.

Hope's back.
What more can I ask?

Black-and-White Sketches

My world is burning like my palms.
The winter's thawing,
coupling moistly,
freshly breeding bubbles and fish.

A dog will come cringing
as if in eternal shame.
A waste of shattered brick in the distance.
Nearby, the odorless city,
trickling thin white clouds of steam
into the fields.

It's going to sneeze.
So what? Let the fields swell
till they press against the sky.
Go on, sneeze—
your nostrils are twitching.

To cease is to be a stone,
or a little beast
that slinks through dark graveyards.
Ceasing, the sea-birds fall like snow,
the lilacs tremble in the gathering dark.

When I Blink

In those misguided years I had such "hallucinations."

I'm convinced.
I try to stare with steady eyes.
I pause by a shimmering fountain,
glancing shyly at bypassers.
When I blink, the fountain turns
into a disembodied snake.

I rest in the temple,
quietly whiling away the time.
The bell turns when I blink
into a bottomless well.

Blossoming on the screeen,
nodding cheerfully in the breeze,
the red flowers turn when I blink
into a steaming pool of blood.
Holding fast to my convictions,
I try to stare at it without blinking.

Yesterday

Yesterday
coils in the corner
like a black snake.
Cold while it lived,
it's colder dead.
Once it crept slowly
over so many hearts,
leaving a greenish trail,
concealing every
trace of blood.

It's dead at last,
secretly buried under
mountains of newsprint.
Now hordes of characters
swarm like ants,
debating how
to circumvent
the second coming.

JIANG HE

Unfinished Poem

1. AN OLD STORY

I stood nailed to a prison wall.
From every side,
from every night since the world began,
black time gathered like a skyful of crows
to peck the heroes to death,
one by one, on the wall.

Their agony had turned to stone,
lonelier than mountains,
to be hacked into shape
for the sake of a nation.

The heroes were nailed to the stone.
The wind eroded them, the rain beat down,
leaving only a semblance—
dismembered arms, hands, faces.
Whips lashed, darkness pecked away
while the old ones labored quietly with their hands,
to build themselves into the wall.

I'm back now, protesting with my death
the shackles of fate.
I'll thrash down fragments,
I'll shake the silent dead till they stand up and shout.

2. GRIEF

I'm a mother. My daughter is going to be shot.
The muzzle of the gun approaches like a black sun
gliding across the arid earth.
I'm an ancient twisted tree. I'm a clutch of dead fingers.

My withered lips are trembling,
grieving with the earth over this disaster.
My heart is flung to the earth
onto my daughter's spattered blood.
Childish tears boil down my cheeks.
I can taste the salt.

The frozen streams have given off singing
as though it were winter.
I'm a sister, a daughter, a wife.
Those aren't leaves—
they're my torn garments, falling.

Waves crash on the rocks
of that raging sea, my hair.
I'm a father, a husband, a son.
My hands thrash the water till my joints creak.
I'm a fleet of ships.
I'm a leveled forest teeming with irrepressible growth.

3. BRIEF LYRIC

As into a dream
I enter the world
like a girl. I run through it
barefoot, my shadow
flowing across
the creaking cobbles.
Fresh drops of blood
mingle with the dew,
bright red agates
on a heaving breast.
A warm green heart
is about to blossom.
I offer my barely
tasted youth

in protest. My arms
reach out for the sun
like frail white arches.
I fear no longer
the trembling stars
in the water. Searching
for night through a forest
of books, I've become
a star myself,
trembling no longer.

4. EXECUTION

Windows are closed, eyes shut against the insidious wind,
but someone's being shot.
I can't hide any longer. My blood won't let me.
The children of the dawn won't let me.

They've thrown me into prison.
Handcuffs and shackles bite into my flesh,
my back's a net of bloody lashes.
They've cut my vocal cords clean through—
but my heart's a ball of fire.
The words burn quietly on my lips.

On this momentous night
in this dark corner of the world,
marching toward the firing squad,
defiant, having no other choice, I choose the sky.
They can't defile the sky.

That the darkness be hidden, I must be shot.
Born in darkness, I still bear a glimmer of light.
That the lies be hidden, I must be shot.
I protest everything light can't endure—
even silence.

Around me people are rounded up,
herded together, deprived of the light.
Surrounded by them, I have become them,
tormented by ancient laws,
attending my own execution,
watching my life spurt out to the last bright drop.

5. UNFINISHED POEM

I'm dead. The bullet holes
gape in my flesh like hollow sockets.
I'm dead, not so people may grieve,
not so flowers may bloom lonely on my grave.
The grief of the people is deep enough already.
Every day the plains are drenched with dew.
Every day rivers stream down to the sea
like an ancient deluge of tears.
Haven't there been occasions enough for grief?

I've been nailed to death on the wall.
The corner of my jacket flutters gently
like a rising flag.

Dividing the Sky

Pan-gu crouched up there
like an ancient bow
drawn taut by time.
Days passed,
turbid, cryptic, interminable.

A great black clam gasped open.
Slowly a limp string tautened and began to quiver.
Slowly Pan-gu's breast grew broader, blue as a gloomy sky.
His heart soon left him.

In the morning he woke with a distant look,
waves of pure light all around him—ten thousand miles
of spindrift, islands, a foaming honeycomb
singing sweetly in the sun.

But the earth was so shapeless.

He bowed himself over the ocean as over a table
attending wordless sails and the gusty gutturals of wind.
On reefs of coral, fish swallowing other fish
thrashed madly inside him.
Cast up on the beaches, seaweed sprawled
like disheveled thoughts half-buried in sand,
like nestlings hatched among pebbles here and there.

He longed for gulls to plunge down
and pluck him to rags,
to soar up once again and bear him across the sky.
Then waves broke over his dream.
Arms that once pillowed the sun now scattered his thoughts.
Tiny clouds swarmed toward land.

Inky cinders streamed down rivers and cataracts,
wind roared through the pines.
Drawing up to his chin a snow-field
marked with his lonely footprints,
Pan-gu drifted to sleep while the moon foretold a heavenly spring.

Chasing the Sun

The day Kua-fu set out he was already old.
Why else would he have thought to chase the sun?
The sun was youth itself.
The day he set out he made all the sacrifices.
Once again he felt the blood glowing within him,
heard drums beating in the earth, in his blood, in the sky.
Standing alone, he chanted softly. Turning, stepping to the east
and the west, he danced a long, long time.

After the rites came a time of perpetual trickery.
He coiled up a serpent and hung it from his ear,
uncoiled it once more, playing like one possessed.
But the sun grew tired of being alone.

Flickering from the serpent's mouth, a tongue of flame
sent childhood memories racing through Kua-fu's heart.

They say he drank up the Yellow River and the Wei.
As a matter of fact, he carried them up to the sun.
As a matter of fact, time and again he and the sun had gone drinking
    together.
Afterwards he washed, then dried himself in the sun,
sprawling over rutted lanes and parched lake beds.

The sun fell asleep in his heart and went soft and tender—
so tender it hurt. When Kua-fu touched it his fingers
trembled like sunlight. He'd grown old. It was time to go.
He flung his walking stick into the sky.

Later someone would lift a stick of kindling from the new spring
    grass.
When he raised his eyes he'd see peaches rolling all round him over
    hills and valleys.

MANG KE

These Days

These days are abject and craven,
like people who've been taunted and tortured.
Look how they cringe in the street.

They can never forget how at sundown
an enormous, malevolent fist might reach out,
grab a beautiful day
and drag it off by the hair.

These days are abject and craven,
not like this cold-hearted, sinewy
wind in the street. Look
how brazenly it swaggers through the crowd.

And what of you?
The wind's no great threat today,
but it could knock you over with one blow.

A Fallen Tree

On the branches of a fallen tree
a shroud of snow is melting
like the flesh of a corpse.
It halts me in my tracks,
afraid to come near.

I stand at a distance
staring, staring
until, at last,
when all the snow has melted,
I can see its skeleton on the ground.

After the Night

Softly, you open your door
to let the darkness out,
after lying all night in his arms.
You hear the wheels of morning
rumbling down the street.

You fling open your window
and drive out all the cooped-up dreams,
sweep out the feathers
pleasure shed last night.

You peer at yourself in the mirror.
Your eyes float in their sockets
like two fish after mating,
each one swimming its own way.

Old Age

The wall grows suddenly wrinkled,
like a mirror in which one old man
catches sight of another.
In the room, it's terribly quiet.
No clock, no ticking at all.

It's so quiet. But the old man
seems to be listening.
Maybe when a man grows this old
he can hear time like a butcher
furtively grinding his knife.

He seems to be listening for something.
What can he possibly have heard?

Sorrows

1

Grey earth.
I gaze at you a long time.
I have nothing to say.

2

Oh, the sky!
Is that your breast,
your icy breast?

3

The sun has closed his burning eye.
I want to hold you.
I want to pluck a song for you
on the lute of love.

4

The heart is a precious stone.
The poem is a basket of flowers.
But what are you?
The icy sky.
What are you?
The silent earth.

5

Can't we be a little closer?
Can't I glimpse your flushed and smiling face?
Oh, there it is, flooded with sunset,
fallen petals all around.

6

What a lovely dusk.
Your smile is veiled in a light rouge.

I'll dredge up from my breast for you
my fondest regards.
I'll cast on you my most adoring glance.

7

I'm in the dark.
I can't make out the path.
The moon is out.
She leans against a tremulous young tree.

8

Hello. Is there anything wrong?
Something I can do?
Hello. Where do you live?
May I see you home?

9

No answer,
only echoes.
I call you as loud as I can
and come up empty-handed.

10

The night is lonely.
She bends her head
as if to murmur something.
Night.

11

Of course
your lover
makes certain demands.
Of course
even if you wear the robes of heaven
I'll unbutton the stars.

12

I know how to love
and be loved in return.
But one sad thought occurs to me:
when will all this be gone,
along with me?

13

Oh fate,
where are you leading me?
I'm worn down by sorrows.

14

Pain remains pain
and sweetness sweetness.
Better that you were a dream,
flown off like a bird.

15

Again, fall's come around.
Again, the leaves are fallen.
Again, this desolate path lies underfoot.
Again, sorrows descend.
Again, loneliness strikes.
Again, this darkest moment of the year.

SHU TING

translated by Carolyn Kizer

The Singing Flower

Thanks to your shining my agony has a faint halo.

I.

I am already a singing flower
Upon your breast
Stirred by the breeze of your breath
As the moonlit fields are stirred.

Cover me, please
With your wide palm
For the time being.

II.

Now permit me to dream:
Snow. Huge forest.
Ancient windbell. Slanting tower.
May I ask for a genuine Christmas tree?
Ice skates on its branches,
Fairy tales, magic flutes,
Fireworks vaunting their ardent fountains.
May I rush through the streets laughing loudly?

III.

What has become of my little basket
Heaped with weeds from my Bumper Crop Allotment?
What has become of my old army canteen?
O those thirsty naps under the scaffolding!
The barrettes I never had a chance to wear.
My English exercises: I LOVE YOU LOVE YOU.
My shadow, stretched or shortened under the streetlamp
And my tears
    that flowed so many times, so many times choked back.

And more
And more

Don't ask me
Why I toss lightly in my dreams.
The past, like a cricket in the corner
Whines in its low, persistent voice.

IV.

Permit me a calm dream.
Don't leave me alone.
That short street—so short!
We have been walking for years.

Permit me a quiet dream.
Don't disturb me.
Those wheeling crows that pester us—
Pay no attention if your eyes are clear.

Permit me a dream of absurdity.
Don't laugh at me.
Each day, newly green, I walk into your poem.
Each evening I return to you, bright rose.

Let me have an indecent dream.
Tolerate my tyranny
When I say, You're mine, you are mine!
Don't reproach me, beloved . . .
I even confess my eagerness to see
   A thousand waves of passion
   Drown you a thousand times.

V.

When our heads touch
As if we were on a speeding train to the moon

The world falls back with a shriek.
The avalanche, Time, swirls madly
       then plunges to pieces.

When our eyes meet
Our souls are like a painting on a gallery wall:
Watery sunlight spreads in rings
       across our field,
Luring us deeper, deeper
       into harmony, silence and renewal.

    VI.

Just like this
We sit in the darkness, clasping hands
And let the voice of our love, ever old and new
Pierce our hearts.
No need to stir, even though
An emperor is knocking at the door,

Nevertheless . . .

    VII.

Wait! What is that? What sound
Rouses the scarlet pulsing in my veins?
      Now I am dizzy with love
      On the ever-sober ocean.
What is that? Whose will
Forces open the lids of my soul and body?
   "You must carry the cross on your back
   Every day, and follow me."

    VIII.

The dream, umbrella-shaped, takes off
And flies away, a dandelion gone to seed
In a cratered moonscape.

IX.

Wild plum branch: my passionate love,
You choose the precarious life
On a storm-swept slope
Not the elegant pose in a vase.

Wild swan: my temperament,
You vow to confront winter, unprotected
Even with a bullet wound
Rather than linger in the cage of Spring.

At any rate, my name and my belief
Are entered for the race,
A single runner, to represent my nation.
I have no right to rest.
In the marathon of life
Speed itself is the goal.

X.

Towards heaven
Which will judge me in the end
I lift my head.

Wind may sweep me away
But for my heart I reserve the right
To refuse to be counted among the lucky.

XI.

Raise your lamp, my love,
                and show the way
So that I and my poems may travel far.
Somewhere, beyond this morass, an ideal bell
Rings in the soft night.
Villages, towns, swarm into my arms:

lights flicker and burn.
Let my poems travel with me,
But the tentacles of highways signal: do not pass!
Still I may walk through the fields
Guided by flowers.

XII.

I walk to the square through the zig-zag streets, back
To the pumpkin shack I guarded, the work in the barley fields,
       deep in the desert (of exile).
Life never stops testing me.
On one side, the laurel wreath, the heavy yoke on the other.
But no one knows I am still that stupid girl
       bad at mathematics.
No matter how the great chorus seems to drown me,
You will hear my singular voice.

XIII.

Still I stand
Intrepid, proud, younger than ever!
The bitter storm deep in my heart
But sunshine on my forehead:
My bright, transparent yellow skin,
My clean, luxuriant black hair!

Mother China,
This daughter requires a new name,
She who comes at your call.

XIV.

So call me your birch sapling,
Your little blue star, Mother.
If the bullet comes
Let it strike me first.
I shall slide to the ground from your shoulder

Smiling, with clear eyes.
No tears. Red flowers in the grass.
Blood flaming on its crest.

XV.

My lover, when that time comes
Don't weep
Though there is no one
who flings up her pastel skirts,
who comes through the narrow alley
where cicadas sing like the rain
to knock at your stained-glass window.
Then there will be no wicked hand
to make the alarm clock ring
saying angrily, "On your mark!
Time to get back to work!"
But don't make a statue of me
On a jade pedestal
And never, to the sound of a lone guitar,
Turn back the calendar, page by page.

XVI.

Your post
Is beneath the banner.
The ideal makes pain bright.
This is the final word
I asked the olive tree
To pass to you.

To find me
Follow the pigeons.
Come in the morning.
I'll be in the hearts
Of women and men.
There you'll find
your singing flower.

Assembly Line

In time's assembly line
Night presses against night.
We come off the factory night-shift
In line as we march towards home.
Over our heads in a row
The assembly line of stars
Stretches across the sky.
Beside us, little trees
Stand numb in assembly lines.

The stars must be exhausted
After thousands of years
Of journeys which never change.
The little trees are all sick,
Choked on smog and monotony,
Stripped of their color and shape.
It's not hard to feel for them;
We share the same tempo and rhythm.

Yes, I'm numb to my own existence
As if, like the trees and stars
—perhaps just out of habit
—perhaps just out of sorrow,
I'm unable to show concern
For my own manufactured fate.

Weekend Evening

The wind has lost its mind,
The night has lost its grip
And slides into drunkenness.
Crazy lights on the coast
Shimmer through humid haze.
Wings of wind sweep over us
Trying to persuade us
To take off from this rock.

No, my dearest, no,
The wind alone can't move us.
Don't kiss the scars on my fingers
Or pity me with tears.
But don't dismiss with a smile
The drudgery of our week.
No, my dearest, no.
Cling to the world, or let it go.

Missing You

A multi-colored chart without a boundary;
An equation chalked on the board, with no solution;
A one-stringed lyre that tells the beads of rain;
A pair of useless oars that never cross the water.

Waiting buds in suspended animation;
The setting sun is watching from a distance.
Though in my mind there may be an enormous ocean,
What emerges is the sum: a pair of tears.

Yes, from these vistas, from these depths,
Only this.

Bits of Reminiscence

A toppled wine-cup,
A stone path floating beneath the moon
Where the grass was trampled:
One azalea branch left lying there . . .

Eucalyptus trees begin to spin
In a collage of stars
As I sit on the rusted anchor,
The dizzy sky reflected in my eyes.

A book held up to shut out candlelight;
Fingers lightly at your mouth;
In the fragile cup of silence
A dream, half-illumined, half-obscure.

Fallen Leaves

The moon sets, a sliver of ice
Afloat on the chilly night.
As we walk home, I hear
The whisper of a sigh:
Our mood is not composed
Of worry or grief alone,
The mood that we are in,
But the thought of whirling leaves
Shaken adrift by the wind.
As you walk away I hear
Your footsteps stir in the leaves.

Spring whispers on every side,
But the fallen leaves at our feet,
Remnants of winter's night,
Make us tremble with private thoughts.
We can't even look at each other,
But in Spring's intenser light
Our thoughts unite again.

The years stamp rings in the trees,
The poems of seeds and leaves
Have hundreds, thousands of lines!
But every tree has only
Its individual theme:
I shall never leave the earth
Though I stretch to the freedom of sky.

Tapping at window and door,
Wind whispers where you are:
You walk under the cottonwood tree
As it showers its petals down.

Though the Spring night makes us shiver
You are not cold at heart.

Then I am struck by a thought:
I am a leaf in the soil.
The wind sings my elegy
As I wait peacefully
For the start of a new green dream
To begin the cycle again.

Maple Leaf

Here is a heart-shaped leaf
Picked up by a gentle hand
On a very special hillside
At the edge of a special wood.
It may not mean very much,
This leaf with its trace of frost

But still the leaf reminds me
Of a twilit avenue,
A mind crowded with thoughts
Released on a gentle breath
That scattered from my shoulders
The rays of the setting sun.

Again, on a special evening
That touch alights on me
Having grown heavy with meaning.
This time I can't deny it,
Deny that intimacy.

Now, when the wind rises
I am prompted to turn my head
And listen to you, leaf,
As you quiver on your twig.

Bei Tai-He Beach

I felt like a child of eight that night,
My needs and moods a mystery to me.
You pushed aside the soaking branch
As you led me to the beach,
The gentle wind caressing
The ragged halo of the moon.
Rhythmically, the tide
Receded into darkness.

The glow of your cigarette
Was reflected in your eyes:
A pair of dancing sparks.
With an ironic gesture
You pretended to snuff them out.
Then quickly you turned your back
As if to conceal your thoughts,
And said, in an unsteady voice,

> "What's happened to the ocean?
> We can't see a thing. Look!
> We've come right to the brink."

Please try to recover
Your dignity and pride.
Go back to that cold pedestal
Heavy as a stone.
Let history possess
Your confident public self.

But let me hold the sorrow
Which belongs to you alone.
Let me carry it far south

To a land of gulls and sails
And your unwritten poems,
Where they will be free to grace
The anchorage of the heart.

Gifts

My dream is the dream of a pond
Not just to mirror the sky
But to let the willows and ferns
Suck me dry.
I'll climb from the roots to the veins,
And when leaves wither and fade
I will refuse to mourn
Because I was dying to live.

My joy is the joy of sunlight.
In a moment of creation
I will leave shining words
In the pupils of children's eyes
Igniting golden flames.
Whenever seedlings sprout
I shall sing a song of green.
I'm so simple I'm profound!

My grief is the grief of birds.
The Spring will understand:
Flying from hardship and failure
To a future of warmth and light.
There my blood-stained pinions
Will scratch hieroglyphics
On every human heart
For every year to come.

Because all that I am
Has been a gift from earth.

Also All

In answer to Bei Dao's "All"

Not all trees are felled by storms.
Not every seed finds barren soil.
Not all the wings of dream are broken,
nor is all affection doomed
to wither in a desolate heart.

No, not all is as you say.

Not all flames consume themselves,
shedding no light on other lives.
Not all stars announce the night
and never dawn. Not every song
will drift past every ear and heart.

No, not all is as you say.

Not every cry for help is silenced,
nor every loss beyond recall.
Not every chasm spells disaster.
Not only the weak will be brought to their knees,
nor every soul be trodden under.

It won't all end in tears and blood.
Today is heavy with tomorrow—
the future was planted yesterday.
Hope is a burden all of us shoulder
though we might stumble under the load.

D. F.

Fairy Tales

for Gu Cheng

You believed in your own story,
then climbed inside it—
a turquoise flower.
You gazed past ailing trees,
past crumbling walls and rusty railings.
Your least gesture beckoned a constellation
of wild vetch, grasshoppers, and stars
to sweep you into immaculate distances.

The heart may be tiny
but the world's enormous.

And the people in turn believe—
in pine trees after rain,
ten thousand tiny suns, a mulberry branch
bent over water like a fishing-rod,
a cloud tangled in the tail of a kite.
Shaking off dust, in silver voices
ten thousand memories sing from your dream.

The world may be tiny
but the heart's enormous.

D. F.

YANG LIAN

Nuo-ri-lang

(In Tibet, the god of virility)

1. THE ROLLING WAVE

The mountain is a tiger burning fiercely beside the sea of chaos.
O there is light, the setting sun floods over you, the earth is
    suspended in the sky.

Pirate sails swell into arms, a crag into a breast, an eagle into a heart.
Undulant thickets swallow the shepherd's solitude.
Streamers flutter above the azure, symbols of faith.

Which white cloud do you silently mourn now,
crawling at the foot of time, haunted by dusk?

At the desert's edge, thousands of headstones lie
like derelict plows, turning bronze to earth and blood to rust.
Do you still weep at each peal of thunder?
Year after year the west wind wakes an army of gold miners buried
    in the dunes.
The log road lies in ruins. Now there's no way past the cliffs. The
    mouth of the cave is dark
and the ancient sorcerers' sky sends down once more the riddle of
    the seven lotuses.
O light, O sacred crimson glaze—the dance of fire, the rites of fire,
the tenderness that washes away the pain, that lends to heaven the
    peace of shattered urns.
Are you shaken by this enormous moment?
The sun waits raptly for the doom to fall.

2. THE GOLDEN TREE

I am the god of cataracts, of snowy peaks,
enormous, potent, overlord of rivers,
cowing the crescent moon.
Birds build their houses in my shaggy breast.

Rank jungle covers the path to the secret spring.
My passion is a herd of mighty stags.
My desire is the month of March,
intensifying in feverish torment.

I am the golden tree.
Men reap gold from my branches.
I hear the passionate whispers from the abyss
and fill it with my torrents.
I ignore the cowards whimpering around me.

Wanton women, gleaming on the water—
who tempts me to drink?

My gaze holds back the night.
Twelve long hours I keep off the frost from the pomegranate.
Wherever I am, no shadow dare appear.
Each strawberry I touch soars from the earth, a blazing star.
I shall possess you—I, the essential man!

3. THE BLOOD SACRIFICE

Decorate the bleached skulls with crimson patterns. Consecrate them
    to the sun, to war.
Feed my eternal life with infant's blood, the blood of circumcision.
A black crag slashes earth's breast like a dagger and lifts out its heart.
A legion of pennants clatters in the dusk like battle drums.
I come alive, smiling proudly, leading you against death,
writing history with my blood, staining the ruins and the
    ceremonies.
Banish your sorrows, then! Let the cliffs block out the mountain's
    challenge.
Vultures plunge again and again like icy blasts, tearing eyes from
    their sockets.
On the altar of torment, bodies, writhing or sprawling, burst into
    bloom.

Long-lost hope returns astride gnawing hunger, scattering screams
     and praises.
What led you to find the lonely splendor beyond the horizon and
     drain your blood? The glory of facing death is greater than
     death itself.

Sacrifice to me! Forty virgins will sing of your valor,
fasting, vigilant, their skin clear and bronze as a bell.
A noble, barbarous, innocent, evil, immaculate, filthy tide,
my vast memory, my secret streams forth in feverish ecstasy.
The pagoda towers, pointing toward the heavens for the twilit
     mountain peaks.
You are redeemed from blood, on the path to blessedness.

4. GATHA

Despair of hope.
Hope for despair.

Despair is the perfect hope.
Hope is the longest despair.

There need be no beginning to hope.
There need be no end to despair.

Perhaps the call comes but once.
The loudest is silence.

5. CELEBRATION AT MIDNIGHT

Blazing the Trail

Solo: Midnight has fallen. Darkness spreads its tiger pelt, streaked
         with glowing gold. The green's so far away. The fragrant grass
         has stirred us. Dew spatters the sky. Who called us here?
Chorus: So many people. O so many people!

Solo: The constellations have tilted. Our sleep is suffused with the soughing of wind among pines. The breeze caresses strange arms. We huddle together, dreaming of a great, bright bonfire. The children are also sleeping.

Chorus: So many people. O so many people!

Solo: The soul grieves, the soul yearns for space in the leaf-choked darkness. A voice emerges from the giddy silence and melts into moonlight. Is this the light we've been seeking?

Chorus: So many people. O so many people!

Piercing the Flower
Nuo-ri-lang proclaims:
The only path is the transparent path.
The only path is the yielding path.
I say to you, follow that river of tribute.
The sun has set, the blood has thawed.
The spirits of mountain peaks and waterfalls,
women with gleaming smiles and inviting eyes
come dancing from every side, freshly bathed,
to transcend illusion, to share my purity and my truth.

Muffling the Drum
Right now the mountain is a ferocious tiger stroked by a vast
     translucent hand.
Right now the sprawling forest's full of trampled beauty—stern and
     dazzling beauty—
revealing the harmony of the universe to the mountain torrents, to
     the glinting rubble of ruined villages.
Tree roots stride like gigantic feet. Children roam about, laughing.
Lilies-of-the-valley chant of my holiness. I gather my character and
     my dignity from the dead.
My light, even as it fails, brightens your golden summons.
Leave bitterness to the sea, which is never at peace.

Right now, beyond the dark night, beyond oblivion, beyond the
    murmuring dreams and the whispered summons,
from the middle of the world I say to you: live on, my people.
Heaven and earth have been created. The birds are twittering. All
    this is merely a revelation.

DONALD FINKEL is the author of twelve books of poetry, most recently *Selected Shorter Poems* and *The Wake of the Electron*. He was presented the Morton Dauwen Zabel Award by the American Academy and Institute of Arts and Letters and is currently Poet in Residence at Washington University in St. Louis.

CAROLYN KIZER won the Pulitzer Prize for poetry in 1985. Her translations of Chinese poetry have been an integral and highly praised part of her work since the 1960s.

Design by David Bullen
Typeset in Mergenthaler Meridien
and Meridien Medium
by Wilsted & Taylor
Printed by Maple-Vail
on acid-free paper